Ladybird  Readers

Sharks

Series Editor: Sorrel Pitts
Text adapted by Sorrel Pitts
Illustrated by Daniel Howarth
Song lyrics by Pippa Mayfield

LADYBIRD BOOKS

UK | USA | Canada | Ireland | Australia
India | New Zealand | South Africa

Ladybird Books is part of the Penguin Random House group of companies
whose addresses can be found at global.penguinrandomhouse.com.
www.penguin.co.uk   www.puffin.co.uk   www.ladybird.co.uk

Penguin
Random House
UK

First published 2016
Updated version reprinted 2024
006

Copyright © Ladybird Books Ltd, 2016, 2024

The moral rights of the author and illustrator have been asserted

Printed in China

The authorized representative in the EEA is Penguin Random House Ireland,
Morrison Chambers, 32 Nassau Street, Dublin D02 YH68

A CIP catalogue record for this book is available from the British Library

ISBN: 978–0–241–25382–3

All correspondence to:
Ladybird Books
Penguin Random House Children's
One Embassy Gardens, 8 Viaduct Gardens, London SW11 7BW

Sharks

Contents

Picture words

 basking shark

 dwarf lantern shark

 great white shark

 hammerhead shark

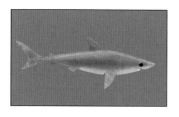 mako shark

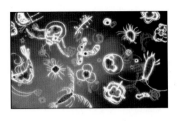

plankton

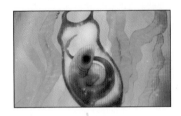

shark egg

shark pups

teeth

Sharks

Many people are frightened of sharks because some sharks are very big and they have big teeth.

great white shark

A shark with big teeth.

But other sharks are small and they have little teeth.

dwarf lantern shark

A small shark with little teeth.

Sharks look for food

Great white sharks eat other big fish and animals.

Sharks are always looking for food.

great white shark

Sharks find food

Many sharks can see very well. This helps them to find other fish to eat.

A hammerhead shark has a very long head.
This helps it to see well.

hammerhead shark

Sharks catch food

Great white sharks often see an animal which they want to eat. Then, they swim very fast to catch it and eat it.

This shark swims very fast!

This shark eats other animals
with its big teeth.

Heads can help

Hammerhead sharks' long heads help them to catch and hold other fish.

hammerhead shark

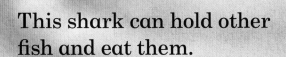

This shark can hold other fish and eat them.

17

Sharks' teeth

Great white sharks have got many teeth. Sometimes a shark loses its teeth, but it soon grows new ones.

A shark can grow many new teeth!

Sharks' bodies

Sharks' long, thin bodies help them to swim fast in the water.

mako shark

This mako shark can swim fast.

Great white sharks' bodies help them to go fast.

great white shark

This shark doesn't swim fast.

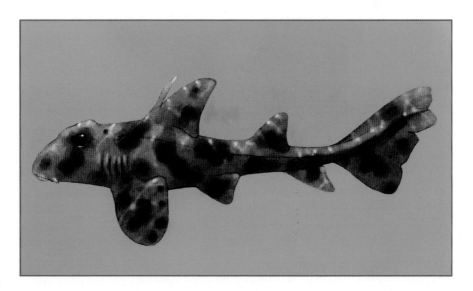

Basking sharks

Basking sharks are very big but they don't eat other fish.

Basking sharks do not eat fish.

basking shark

Eat, eat, eat!

Basking sharks eat very small animals called plankton.

basking shark

Basking sharks don't have big teeth to eat plankton. They catch them in their open mouths.

plankton

Basking sharks' food

Basking sharks need to eat lots of plankton because they are very big.

basking shark

Basking sharks eat lots of little plankton.

plankton

Plankton are very small animals.

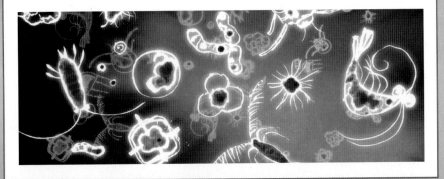

Big and little sharks

Some sharks are big and other sharks are little.

basking shark

Basking sharks are VERY big.

Dwarf lantern sharks are VERY little.

The light-in-the-dark shark!

Dwarf lantern sharks make a light in the sea with their bodies. You can see them swimming in the dark water!

dwarf lantern shark

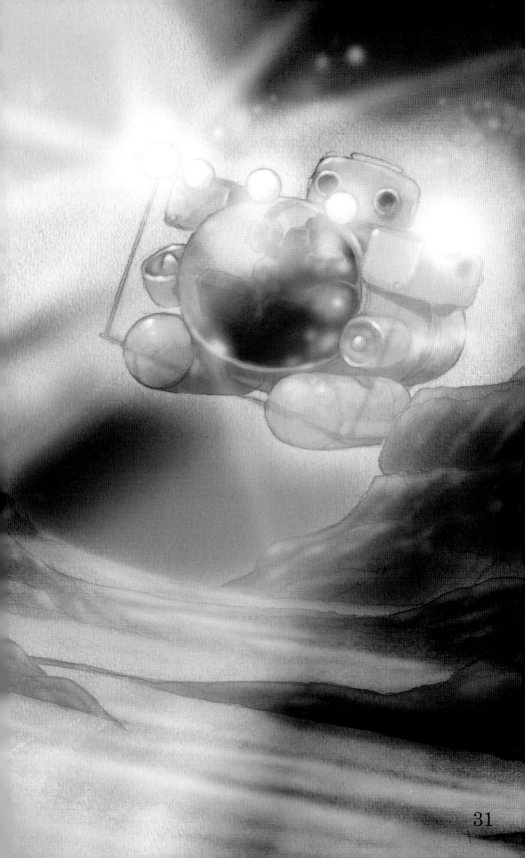

Baby sharks

Baby sharks are called pups.
Some pups come from an egg.

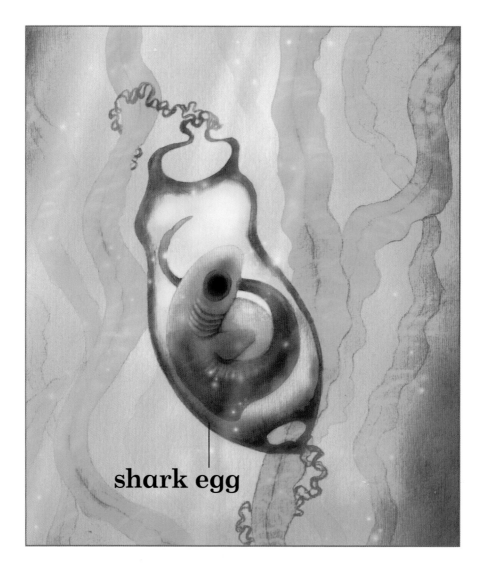

shark egg

This shark pup comes from an egg.

Many shark pups don't come
from eggs. They grow inside
their mothers.

mako shark

shark pup

The mako shark pups live with their mothers.

Pups look after themselves

Shark pups find and eat fish.
Their mothers don't help
them to do this.

shark pup

These mako shark pups
swim and eat fish.

Shark journeys

Some sharks travel
many miles.

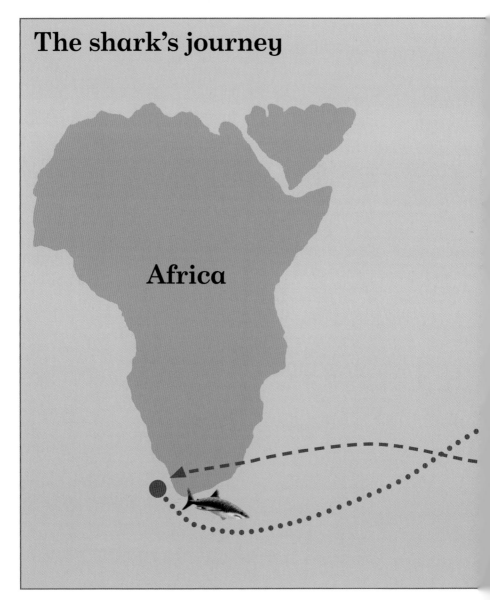

The shark's journey

Africa

A great white shark swam
from Africa to Australia.
And then it swam back!

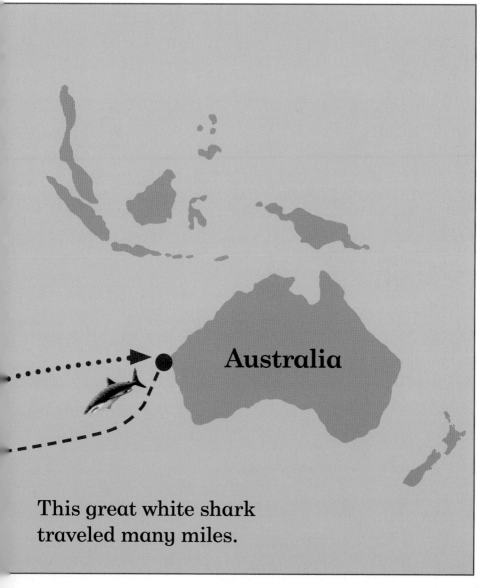

Australia

This great white shark
traveled many miles.

Swim, swim, swim!

Many sharks have to swim all the time. If they don't swim all the time, they die.

These hammerhead sharks
must swim all the time.

Hungry sharks

Many sharks kill and eat other animals. But sharks don't often kill or eat people.

41

Which are your favorite sharks?

great white shark

hammerhead shark

basking shark

dwarf lantern shark

mako shark

Activities

The key below describes the skills practiced in each activity.

Spelling and writing

Reading

Speaking

Listening*

Critical thinking

Singing*

Preparation for the Cambridge Young Learners exams

*To complete these activities, listen to the audio downloads available at **www.ladybirdeducation.co.uk**

1 Match the words to the pictures.

1 basking shark

a

2 dwarf lantern shark

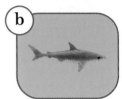
b

3 great white shark

c

4 hammerhead shark

d

5 mako shark

e

2 **Look and read. Choose the correct words and write them on the lines.**

teeth   plankton   pups   egg

1 Some sharks use these to catch fish.   _teeth_

2 Some sharks come from this.   ....

3 Baby sharks are called this.   ....

4 Basking sharks eat these very small animals.   ....

3 **Read the text and circle the correct answers.**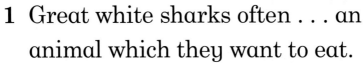

1 Great white sharks often . . . an animal which they want to eat.

   a see

   b sees

2 Then, they . . . very fast to catch it and eat it.

   a swim

   b swimming

3 Sometimes a shark . . . its teeth, but it soon grows new ones.

   a lose

   b loses

4 A shark can . . . many new teeth!

   a to grow

   b grow

4 **Read the answers.**
Write the questions.

1 What kind of shark is it?

It's a hammerhead shark.

2 ....

It lives in the sea.

3 ....

....

It has a long head to help it
catch fish.

5 Talk about the two pictures with a friend. How are they different?

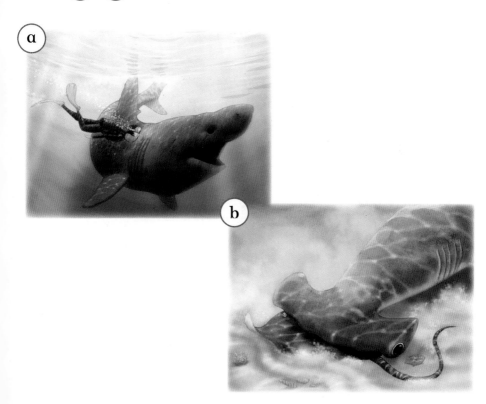

a

b

In picture a, there is one person. There are no people in picture b.

6 Find the words. 📖

plankton
basking
mako
teeth
hammerhead

s m i m p l a n k t o n t e a h a m m e r h e a d s c m a k o c b b a s k i n g d w a t e e t h x t h y

7 **Read the text.**
Choose the right words and write them on the lines. 📖 ✏️ 🏅

1 and	but	because
2 small	smaller	smallest
3 with	or	because
4 had to	has to	need to

Basking sharks are very big,

1 .... but .... they don't eat other fish.

Basking sharks eat very 2 ....

animals called plankton. They catch them

in their open mouths 3 ....

they don't have big teeth. They

4 .... eat lots of plankton.

8 **Read the text. Write some words to complete the sentences.**

> Yesterday, Jack and Jess went swimming in the sea to look for sharks. A basking shark swam next to them, but they didn't see any great white sharks. They watched the basking shark eat plankton, but they didn't swim near the shark's big open mouth!

1 Jack and Jess went swimming in the sea _____yesterday_____.

2 They saw a _____.

3 They didn't want _____

_____ near the shark's mouth!

9 **Circle the correct answers.**

1 Why do basking sharks need to eat lots of plankton?

  a Because they are very big.

  b Because they have a lot of pups.

2 Do dwarf lantern sharks grow big?

  a Yes, they do.

  b No, they don't.

3 What is different about dwarf lantern sharks?

  a They make a light with their bodies.

  b They have big teeth.

10 **Listen, and write the answers.**

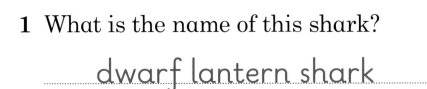

1 What is the name of this shark?

dwarf lantern shark

2 Where does it live?

in the sea near ....

3 What does it eat?

....

4 What color is it?

....

5 What can it do?

make a ....

Circle the correct words.

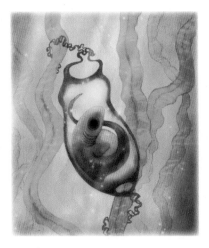 

1 Many shark pups don't come
  by / **from** eggs.

2 They grow **outside** / **inside**
  their mothers.

3 Shark pups look after
  ourselves. / **themselves**.

4 Sharks kill other fish, but they
  often / **don't often** kill people.

12 Circle the correct words.

1 Mako sharks

   a come from an egg.

   b don't come from an egg.

2 The mother mako shark

   a doesn't help her pups to find food.

   b helps her pups to find food.

3 Mako shark pups

   a can't swim.

   b can swim.

4 Mako shark pups eat

   a fish.

   b shark eggs.

13 Look and read. Write *yes* or *no*.

1 Hammerhead sharks
have short heads.   no

2 They swim all the time.   ....

3 Hammerhead sharks die
if they swim all the time.   ....

4 They make a light with
their bodies.   ....

14 Look at the letters.
Write the words.

> **r h a s k**

1 The mako 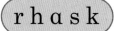 pups swim and eat fish.

> **t v r e l a**

2 Some sharks .... many miles.

> **m s w i**

3 Hammerhead sharks must .... all the time.

> **l l i k**

4 Many sharks .... and eat other fish.

> **l o p p e e**

5 Sharks don't often eat ....

58

15 **Read the questions. Write answers using the words in the box.**

> frightened   big teeth
> hammerhead   dwarf lantern

1 How do many people feel about sharks?

Many people feel frightened about sharks.

2 Which shark is very small?

....

....

3 Which shark has a very long head?

....

....

4 How does the great white shark eat other fish?

....

16 **Circle the correct pictures.**

1 This shark is as small as a pencil.

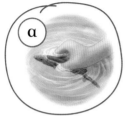 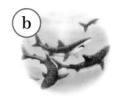 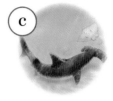

2 Some sharks come out of this.

 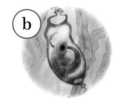 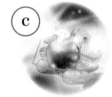

3 Mako shark pups grow inside her.

 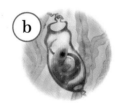 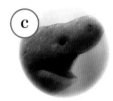

4 This shark makes a light.

 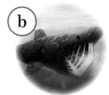 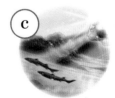

17 Ask and answer the questions with a friend. 🗨 ⬣

1

> Are you frightened of any sea animals?

> No, because they live in the sea.

2 Which sea animal is your favorite? Why?

3 Which shark would you like to see? Why?

4 Would you swim in water with sharks in it? Why? / Why not?

18 **Listen, and ☑ the boxes.** 🎧 ⬤

1 Which is the boy's favorite shark?

(a)  ☐

(b)  ☐

(c) 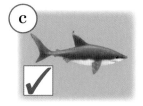 ☑

2 What is the shark doing?

(a) 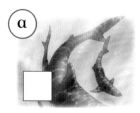 ☐

(b)  ☐

(c) 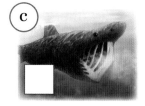 ☐

3 Which picture is the girl talking about?

(a)  ☐

(b) 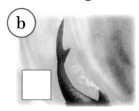 ☐

(c) 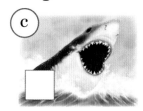 ☐

4 What is this shark better at?

(a) 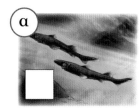 ☐

(b) 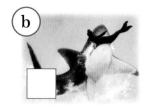 ☐

(c) 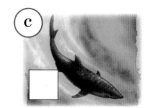 ☐

19 Sing the song. 🎵

A little fish said, "I'm afraid of sharks!
Great whites and hammerheads
are bigger than me!"
I told the fish, "And they're faster, too!
But there are lots of different
sharks in the sea.

Do not be afraid! That's a basking shark!
It is very, very big. But what does it eat?
Lots and lots of plankton,
which are very, very small.
There are lots of different
sharks in the sea.

Do not be afraid! That's a dwarf
lantern shark.
It is very, very small.
And look, can you see?
A light in the water that its body makes.
There are lots of different sharks
swimming in the sea."

Visit www.ladybirdeducation.co.uk
for more FREE Ladybird Readers resources

- ✓ Digital edition of every title
- ✓ Audio tracks (US/UK)
- ✓ Answer keys
- ✓ Lesson plans

- ✓ Role-plays
- ✓ Classroom display material
- ✓ Flashcards
- ✓ User guides

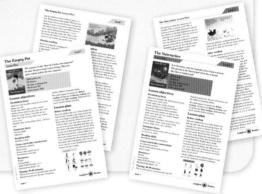

Register and sign up to the newsletter to receive your FREE classroom resource pack!